DAY YOM יוֹם

WEEK sha-VOO-ah שָׁבוּעַ

YEAR sha-NAH שָׁנָה

MONTH KHO-desh חוֹדֶשׁ

SHABBAT

TEVET SHEVAT ADAR NISAN IYAR SIVAN TAMUZ AV ELUL TISHREI KHESHVAN KISLEV

THURSDAY FRIDAY SUNDAY MONDAY TUESDAY WEDNESDAY

In loving memory of my mother,
Rose Heringman Sper.

—E.S.

A special thanks to Mark Meretzky whose knowledge of everything
is astounding, and to the many wise people in my world who gave
me valuable feedback—Jennifer Barber, Irv Dunn, Orit Kent,
Carmine Fantasia, Linda Falken, Jacqueline Fleischman, Matan Lakein,
Amy Rosenthal, Jane Sper, and Rabbi Toba Spitzer.

All About Jewish Time

2006 First published as *The Kids' Fun Book of Jewish Time*

ISBN 978-0-9980733-1-6

Printed in the USA

Published by Jump Press
www.jumppress.com

ALL ABOUT
Jewish Time

Emily Sper

JUMP | PRESS

BOSTON

Did you know there are different ways to count days, weeks, months, and years?

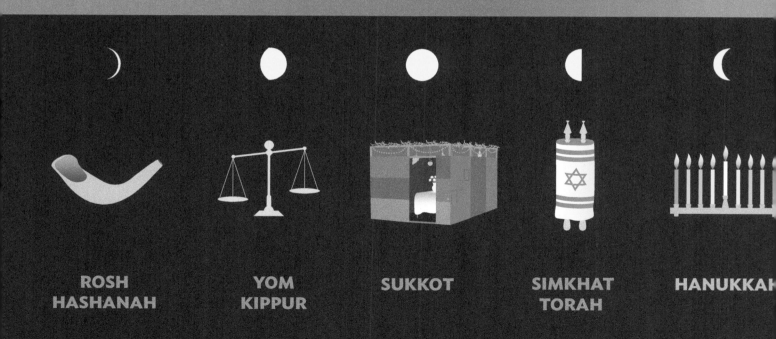

ROSH HASHANAH

YOM KIPPUR

SUKKOT

SIMKHAT TORAH

HANUKKAH

Jewish holidays follow a special calendar— the Hebrew calendar.

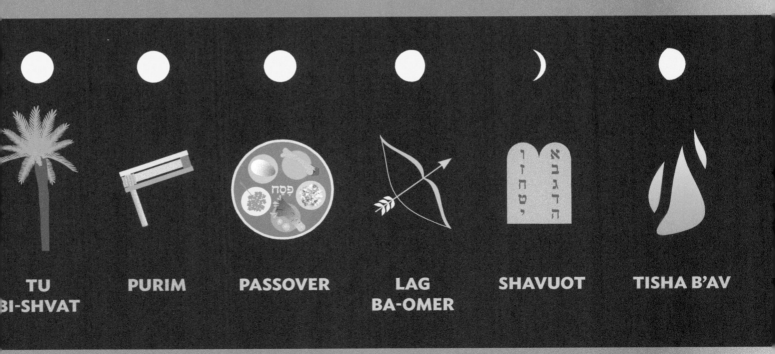

TU BI-SHVAT

PURIM

PASSOVER

LAG BA-OMER

SHAVUOT

TISHA B'AV

Our ancestors spoke Hebrew. That's why the Jewish holidays have Hebrew names.

We read and write Hebrew from right to left. Alef is the first letter of the Hebrew alphabet.

Sound	Name	Letter
l	lamed	ל
m	mem	ם or מ
n	nun	ן or נ
s	samekh	ס
silent	ayin	ע
p	pey	פ
f	fey	ף or פ
tz	tzadee	ץ or צ
k	kof	ק
r	resh	ר
sh	shin	שׁ
s	sin	שׂ
t	tav	ת

ALPHABET

silent	alef	א
b	bet	ב
v	vet	ב
g, as in go	gimel	ג
d	dalet	ד
h	hey	ה
v	vav	ו
z	zayin	ז
kh	khet	ח
t	tet	ט
y	yod	י
k	kaf	כ
kh	khaf	ן or כ

HEBREW VOWELS

- **a** or **ah**, as in **father**
- **a** or **ah**, as in **father**
- **ai**, as in **eye**
- **e** or **eh**, as in **pet**
- **ee**, as in **bee**
- **ey**, as in **they**
- **o**, as in **go** (above the letter vav)
- **o**, as in **go** (to the upper left of letter)
- **oo**, as in **moo** (next to the letter vav)
- **oo**, as in **moo**

kh: Try to say "huh" while clearing your throat. If you can't say "**khai**," the Hebrew word for life, say "**hai**," and keep practicing!

Numbers

Hebrew letters are also numbers.

$$\boldsymbol{\aleph\text{'}} = \boldsymbol{\aleph} + \boldsymbol{\text{'}}$$

11   1   10

Like the 4th of July, the names of some Jewish holidays are a number and a month. Tu bi-Shvat is the 15th day of the month of Shevat.

$$\boldsymbol{\mathrm{טו}} = \boldsymbol{\mathrm{ו}} + \boldsymbol{\mathrm{ט}}$$

15   6   9

Thousands of years ago, when the Hebrew calendar was invented, the moon, the sun, and the stars were the clocks and calendars.

stars

כּוֹכָבִים

ko-kha-VEEM

moon

יָרֵחַ

ya-REY-akh

Hebrew days are counted from sunset to sunset.

sun
שֶׁמֶשׁ
SHEH-mesh

sunset sh'kee-AH שְׁקִיעָה

day

יוֹם

YOM

night

לַיְלָה

LAI-la

morning
בֹּקֶר
BO-ker

evening
עֶרֶב
EH-rev

After the sun
goes down,
it is evening,
the beginning
of a new day.

In the beginning...
בְּרֵאשִׁית
b'rey-SHEET

The Torah tells us it took God six days to create the world. On the seventh day, God stopped working and rested. That's why the week has seven days.

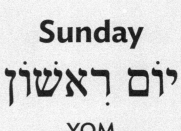

Sunday

יוֹם רִאשׁוֹן

YOM
ree-SHON

1 א

Monday

יוֹם שֵׁנִי

YOM
shey-NEE

2 ב

Tuesday

יוֹם שְׁלִישִׁי

YOM
shlee-SHEE

3 ג

4

ד

Wednesday

יוֹם רְבִיעִי

YOM
r'vee-EE

5

ה

Thursday

יוֹם חֲמִישִׁי

YOM
kha-mee-SHEE

6

ו

Friday

יוֹם שִׁשִּׁי

YOM
shee-SHEE

week

שָׁבוּעַ

sha-VOO-AH

The days of the Hebrew
week are named "First Day"
through "Sixth Day."
And the seventh day is…

Shabbat

שַׁבָּת

sha-BAT

The week ends with Shabbat, the "Day of Rest." Shabbat is the only Jewish holiday that comes every week.

Is it Shabbat or Shabbos? Both are correct. "Shabbat" is Hebrew and "Shabbos" is Yiddish. In English, you can also say "the Sabbath."

Evening
of Shabbat
עֶרֶב שַׁבָּת

EH-rev sha-BAT

On Friday, just before the sun sets, we light candles to welcome Shabbat.

candles

נֵרוֹת

ney-ROT

We begin Shabbat dinner by saying blessings over the wine (or grape juice) and challah.

challah

חַלָּה

kha-LAH

**blessing
over wine**

קִדּוּשׁ

kee-DOOSH

בּוֹרֵא פְּרִי הַגָּפֶן

Day of Shabbat

יוֹם הַשַּׁבָּת

YOM ha-sha-BAT

On Shabbat, we stop and take a deep breath. We are thankful for all we have.

Every week, there is a new story to read in the Torah.

Shabbat is over when we can see the first three stars in the evening sky.

Havdalah

הַבְדָּלָה

hav-da-LAH

The Havdalah ceremony marks the end of Shabbat and the beginning of the new week. We say blessings over the wine, Havdalah candle, and spices.

בּוֹרֵא פְּרִי הַגָּפֶן

fruit of the vine

פְּרִי הַגָּפֶן

p'REE ha-GA-fen

Against the light of the flame, our hands make shadows and our fingernails shine.

We think about night and day, Shabbat and the week to come.

light of fire

מְאוֹרֵי הָאֵשׁ

me'o-REY ha-EYSH

The Havdalah spice box smells sweet. We bring the sweetness of Shabbat into the new week.

various spices

מִינֵי בְשָׂמִים

mee-NEY v'sa-MEEM

We see more and more of the moon until it is full, then less and less until we can no longer see it.

month

חֹדֶשׁ

KHO-desh

Each Hebrew month begins when we see the first sliver of the moon after not seeing it at all. And on the 15th day, there is a full moon.

A month has 29 or 30 days.

To every thing there is a season, and a time for every experience under heaven.

—Ecclesiastes (Kohelet) 3:1

every thing

הַכֹּל

ha-KOL

season

זְמַן

z'MAN

time

עֵת

EYT

heaven

שָׁמַיִם

sha-MA-yeem

1
Nisan
נִיסָן

nee-SAN

2
Iyar
אִיָּר

ee-YAR

3
Sivan
סִיוָן

see-VAN

4
Tamuz
תַּמּוּז

ta-MOOZ

5
Av
אָב

AV

6
Elul
אֱלוּל

eh-LOOL

7
Tishrei
תִּשְׁרֵי

teesh-REY

8
Kheshvan
חֶשְׁוָן

khesh-VAN

9
Kislev
כִּסְלֵו

kees-LEYV

10

Tevet

טֵבֵת

tey-VEYT

11

Shevat

שְׁבָט

sh'VAT

12

Adar

אֲדָר

ah-DAR

year

שָׁנָה

sha-NAH

The months of the year are counted from Nisan, the first month of spring, through Adar, the last month of winter.

Calendar years are counted from Tishrei, the first month of autumn, through Elul, the last month of summer.

The year has 12 months, except in a leap year when an extra month is added after Adar.

1 Tishrei
Rosh Hashanah
רֹאשׁ הַשָּׁנָה
ROSH ha-sha-NAH

25 Kislev
Hanukkah
חֲנֻכָּה
kha-noo-KAH

15 Nisan
Passover
פֶּסַח
PE-sakh

10 Tishrei

Yom Kippur

יוֹם כִּפּוּר

YOM kee-POOR

15 Tishrei

Sukkot

סֻכּוֹת

soo-KOT

23 Tishrei

Simkhat Torah

שִׂמְחַת תּוֹרָה

seem-KHAT to-RAH

15 Shevat

Tu bi-Shvat

ט"וּ בִּשְׁבָט

too beesh-VAT

14 Adar

Purim

פּוּרִים

poo-REEM

holidays

חַגִּים

kha-GEEM

18 Iyar

Lag ba-Omer

ל"ג בָּעֹמֶר

LAG ba-O-mer

6 Sivan

Shavuot

שָׁבוּעוֹת

sha-voo-OT

9 Av

Tisha b'Av

תִּשְׁעָה בְּאָב

tee-SHAH b'AV

Days of Awe

יָמִים נוֹרָאִים

ya-MEEM no-ra-EEM

On the first day of the month of Tishrei, we celebrate the New Year on Rosh Hashanah.

We call the 10 days between Rosh Hashanah and Yom Kippur the "Days of Awe."

עוד יבוא שלום עלינו

Head of the Year

Day of Atonement

Five days later, we celebrate Sukkot, and on the last day of Sukkot, Simkhat Torah.

Festival of Booths

זֶה לֹא הַתּוֹרָה הָאֲמִתִּית
אֶלָא טִפְשָׁט שֶׁיְמַלָא א
הַחֵלֶל וִירְאֶה כְמוֹ הַ
הָאֲמִתִּיָּא אַף אֶל תֵּרָא
סַפֵיר אָמִילִי אֲחוֹת שֶׁ
בַּת שֶׁל רָחֵל וְרָאִי אֶב
שֶׁל שָׂרָה וּרְבָּיד וְלַם
הֻגְמְרָה שֶׁל לָרָה וְפֵר
זֶה לֹא הַתּוֹרָה הָאֲמִתִּית
אֶלָא טִפְשָׁט שֶׁיְמַלָא א
הַחֵלֶל וִירְאֶה כְמוֹ הַ
הָאֲמִתִּיָּא אַף אֶל תֵּרָא
סַפֵיר אָמִילִי אֲחוֹת שֶׁ
בַּת שֶׁל רָחֵל וְרָאִי אֶב
שֶׁל שָׂרָה וּרְבָּיד וְלַם
הֻגְמְרָה שֶׁל לָרָה וְפֵר
זֶה לֹא הַתּוֹרָה הָאֲמִתִּית
אֶלָא טִפְשָׁט שֶׁיְמַלָא א
הַחֵלֶל וִירְאֶה כְמוֹ הַ
הָאֲמִתִּיָּא אַף אֶל תֵּרָא
סַפֵיר אָמִילִי אֲחוֹת שֶׁ
בַּת שֶׁל רָחֵל וְרָאִי אֶב
שֶׁל שָׂרָה וּרְבָּיד וְלַם
הֻגְמְרָה שֶׁל לָרָה וְפֵר
זֶה לֹא הַתּוֹרָה הָאֲמִתִּית
אֶלָא טִפְשָׁט שֶׁיְמַלָא א
הַחֵלֶל וִירְאֶה כְמוֹ הַ

Joy of Torah

Would you believe it takes a whole year to read the Torah?

On Simkhat Torah, we start over again at the beginning.

In the first story, God creates the world.

rain

גֶּשֶׁם

GEH-shem

In Ancient Israel, wheat and barley seeds were planted before the windy, rainy winter. Seeds need rain to sprout.

HANKKAH

Festival of Lights

PURIM

Queen Esther Saves the Jews

TU BI-SHVAT

The Israelites waited until a tree was three years old before picking its fruit. Having a birthday for trees helped them keep track of the age of a tree or crop.

Almond trees are the first plants to blossom after the winter rains. That's when we celebrate Tu bi-Shvat.

New Year of Trees

Days of the Omer

The harvest of wheat and barley was counted between Passover and Shavuot.

 **PASSOVER**

LAG BA-OMER

SHAVUOT

Freedom from Slavery

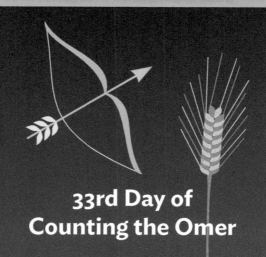

33rd Day of Counting the Omer

Receiving of the 10 Commandments

We begin counting the 49 "Days of the Omer" on the 2nd day of Passover, celebrate Lag ba-Omer on the 33rd day, and then, on the 50th day, it's Shavuot.

ז 7	ו 6	ה 5	ד 4	ג 3	ב 2	א 1
יד 14	יג 13	יב 12	יא 11	י 10	ט 9	ח 8
כא 21	כ 20	יט 19	יח 18	יז 17	טז 16	טו 15
כח 28	כז 27	כו 26	כה 25	כד 24	כג 23	כב 22
לה 35	לד 34	לג 33	לב 32	לא 31	ל 30	כט 29
מב 42	מא 41	מ 40	לט 39	לח 38	לז 37	לו 36
מט 49	מח 48	מז 47	מו 46	מה 45	מד 44	מג 43

ISRAEL INDEPENDENCE DAY

May 14, 1948
5 Iyar

dew

טַל

TAL

Summers were hot and dry. It never rained. But dew, droplets of water that form at night, kept plants alive.

In the summer, grapes ripen. Thousands of years ago, people made juice and wine from grapes. We still do!

On Tisha b'Av, we remember the destruction of the Temple in Jerusalem.

Every day of the week, month, and year, we try to make the world a better place in which to live.

Teach us to count our days so **we may gain a heart of wisdom.** —Psalm 90

We smile. We love.
We listen. We help others.
We tell the truth.
We share. We forgive.

לִמְנוֹת יָמֵינוּ כֵּן הוֹדַע וְנָבִא לְבַב חָכְמָה.

leem-NOT ya-MEY-noo KEYN ho-DAH v'na-VEE l'VAV khokh-MAH.

forever

לְעוֹלָם

l'o-LAM

CPSIA information can be obtained
at www.ICGtesting.com
Printed in the USA
LVHW070506170322
713684LV00008B/129